Guilty

Law & Order

Pat Durden Johnson

Guilty

This book is a work of fiction. The characters, locales, incidents, or persons portrayed are fictitious. Any similarity to real persons, living or dead, is purely coincidental and not intended by the author. This is a product of the author's imagination.

For ordering, booking, permission, or questions, contact the author please visit www.authorklap.com or email keycitypro@gmail.com

Publisher: KeyCity Publishing

ISBN: 9798987842294

Book Cover: It Takes Faith Media

Interior Photos: Christian Seymore, Canva, & Pixabay

Dedication

Dedicated to the Guardians of Society: To the tireless protectors of our communities, our law enforcement officers, whose bravery and dedication safeguard our streets. And to Judge John Morse, Judge Judy Sheindlin, and Judge Frank Caprio. And to the steadfast leaders of faith, whose guidance and compassion nourish our souls. Your unwavering commitment to service and justice inspires us all.

Acknowledgments

I would like to thank Dr. Apostle Kenneth Karl Law of The Embassy Church in Fleming, GA, for saying there were more books within me to write. His prophecy was later confirmed by Apostle Mistry Holmes Dorsey. As she spoke God's Word for books to come forth, this book was born during Kingdom Momentum 2024. Other prophecies also came forth, "Write the Vision and Make it Plain."

Thanks to my beloved cousin Dr. Dexter Earl Marks for the time proofreading and profound insights. PhD Dexter Earl Marks, a college professor in the English Department at New York State University and Savannah State University.

And a humble thanks to my spiritual mother, Dr. LaWanda R. Law's prayers, my beloved husband and children, and friends who believed in me and encouraged me to complete the project The Holy Spirit has designed.

I express my deepest gratitude to my granddaughter Christian Seymore whose expertise and dedication have significantly enhanced this project with a Bachelor of Fine Arts in Sequential Art. Christian Seymore has masterfully illustrated the principles of Law and Order, bringing clarity and depth to complex concepts through her exceptional artistry. Her unique ability to merge art with legal principles has not only made this work visually compelling but also intellectually stimulating. Thank you for your invaluable contribution and unwavering support. With warm regards to my granddaughter, Christian Seymore, I extend my heartfelt congratulations on your graduation in Fine Arts from SCAD and your remarkable work as an Art Teacher with SCCPSS. Your exceptional drawing has significantly enhanced this Teacher Manual, bringing beauty and inspiration to its pages. Your dedication and artistic talent are truly appreciated, and I am grateful for your invaluable contribution.

Last, to my book cover designer Mrs. Simone Bryant, and my photographer Keaf Avant.

Table of Contents

Preface

GUILTY: LAW & ORDER

 This book is for everyone looking for justice for themselves or a loved one. After sharing my study of various criminal cases, biblically, I realized this book could encourage others to believe in justice.

After studying the various biblical crimes carried out by those in more affluent sections of society such as King Ahab, King David, King Herod, and Judge Samson, also the crimes committed by persons of high social status and respectability in the course of their occupation, Noah (Ham), Achan, Queen Jezebel, Queen Herodias, Jacob's sons, and Ananias and Sapphira ranged in the categories; these crimes are motivated by the same forces driving other criminals. Years ago, crimes focused on violators rather than the offense.

However, today the focus has shifted to the nature of the crime, rather than the persons or occupations involved. These crimes denote a display of fake schemes, corruption, and commercial offenses committed by leaders, businessmen, and public officials alike. Its current usage includes a broad range of nonviolent offenses where cheating, dishonesty, and corruption are the central elements of the crime. Violation of the criminal law committed by a person of responsibility and high social status in the course of one's occupation.

On the other hand, in a world often fixated on the sensational crimes of the streets, it's easy to overlook the quieter yet equally devastating offenses that are perpetrated in corridors of power.

This book delves into an intricate web of white-collar crime, shining a light on the individuals in positions of privilege and influence who betray trust and manipulate systems for personal gain. Corporate fraud to political corruption undermine the very fabric of society, eroding trust and exacerbating inequalities.

Through meticulous research and analysis, this book seeks to unravel the complexities of these offenses, offering insights into their motivations, mechanisms, and societal implications. It is a call to action for greater transparency, accountability, and justice in all spheres of power.

On the other hand, SIN usually involves two or more people. Sinners refer to those whose behavior was considered outside of the law in an open and obvious way. We fool ourselves if we think our sin affects only us. Disobedience brings ruin even to the innocent. Sin's effects go beyond the initial sinner. It leads us to think that our happiness and fulfillment lie in something other than God and a loving community with others. "Therefore, we should decimate every moment, every desire, every thought act, every power and impulse of our soul to God and His love." - St. Frances Sales

The main motivations for crime are sex, money, addiction, and emotions.

Never mistake law for justice as an idea. Law is a tool. Justice is merely incidental to law and order. An unjust law is a code that's out of harmony with moral law. When law and morality contradict each other, the citizen has the cruel alternative of losing respect for the law.

"A just law is a manmade code that squares with moral law or the law of God." - Martin Luther King

Law and Order can be succinctly defined as the system of rules and regulations established by a governing authority to maintain peace, enforce justice, and uphold the lights and responsibility of individuals within a society.

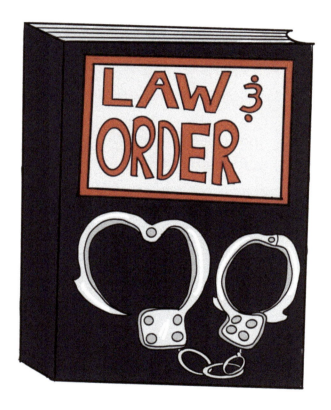

Open Arguments

Your honor, and Ladies and Gentlemen of the jury, today we're going to present ten cases to you that delve into the depths of human nature and the consequences of sin. We will unveil the truth behind a series of actions that have led to harm, betrayal, and the unraveling of trust.

Through our evidence, witnesses, and testimonies, we vigorously aim to shed light on the darkness that often accompanies sin, and ultimately seek justice for those who have been wronged.

We will unveil tales of deceptions and revelations. Through meticulous examinations of the evidence, we will reveal how the defendants succumbed to temptation, committing acts of sin in secrecy. The truth cannot stay hidden forever. Through the relentless pursuit of justice, we've uncovered the veils of deceit committed and brought them to the light of accountability. No Matter How Committed Sin Will Be Exposed! Everything started in the Garden of Eden.

CASE #1 - Innocence – Adam and Eve

- Sin, quilt, and neurosis are the same, fruit of the TREE of KNOWLEDGE.
- Ignorance is not innocence but sin. Nothing in all the world is more dangerous than sincere ignorance and conscientious stupidity.
- For me sin is not a stain that I have to clean, what I should do is ask pardon and make a reconciliation, not stop at the cleaners on my way home.
- Feeling like a sinner is one of the most beautiful things that can happen to a person if it leads him/her to the ultimate consequences of reconciliation.
- Fear mismanaged leads to sin and sin leads to hiding. Since we've all sinned, we all hide, not in bushes, but in eighty-hour workweeks, temper tantrums, and religious busyness. We avoid contact with God.

Case #1: Adam & Eve

KINGDOM OF GOD COURT

Tree of Good & Evil	District of	Garden of Eden

Kingdom of God	vs	Judgement in a Criminal Case

Adam & Eve		#1

Title & Section	Nature of Offense	Count
Gen Ch. 2 & 3	Disobedience to God	1

CASE DOCKET #1 – Innocence: Adam and Eve

Innocent — God does not wink at innocent anymore. We are in the era of conscience.

Then the prosecuting attorney begins to speak to present his case.

It is written in Isaiah, "I am God, and there is none like me. I declare from the beginning how it will end and foretell from the start when it has not yet happened. Be Ye Holy For I Am Holy!

<u>Text</u>: Genesis 2nd and 3rd Chapters
Adam and Eve: Sloth/Reluctance

<u>The LAW</u>: (It is written) God commanded them, Thou shalt not eat of the tree of knowledge of good and evil.

<u>Sin</u>: Disobedience enters into the atmosphere and the environment in the Garden of Eden. The Old Testament tells of Adam and Eve, our progenitors, they lived in paradise in total INNOCENCE until the serpent (the devil) enticed them to eat the forbidden fruit from the tree of knowledge. As a punishment for their obedience, God banished them from paradise.

<u>How Sin Was Committed</u>: They drifted into sinful thought because of the mystery of deception. "The serpent deceived me, and I ate" (Genesis 3:13). One should be clear that when she thought the fruit was 'desirable', she already sinned, in her thoughts. The bait was, "You surely won't die." Those words were spoken by the serpent. Eve

succumbed to the serpent's temptation. She ate from the tree and made sure that Adam did as well. Their eyes were opened, and they knew that they were naked (Genesis 3:7). For this transgression, they were evicted from paradise.

How Sin Was Exposed: The eyes of both of them were opened, and they knew that they were NAKED (Genesis 3:7). God called out to Adam. "Where art thou?" They hid from God due to being ashamed and knowing they were naked. For succumbing to temptation and eating the fruit of the forbidden tree of knowledge of good and evil, God confronted them for their sin. God clothed them with skin cloth when they were naked in the garden after eating the forbidden fruit. They were guilty and felt ashamed. Trying to hide sin from God is like running from your shadow you can never get away from. You cannot run away from God because He knows everything and is everywhere.

Evidence: Adam and Eve ate a negative thought (was it a negative thought or a lie) (you won't surely die) causing them to become uncovered with God's glory. They thought no more as God. Their intellectual mind spoke about being naked after eating from the Tree of Knowledge then used fig leaves to cover themselves.

<u>Judgment</u>: By their sin, as the first family, they lost the original holiness they had received from God, not only for themselves but for all humans. Adam and Eve transmitted to their descendants human nature, wounded by their first sin, hence deprived of original holiness and justice; this deprivation all led to the 'original sin.' God banished them from the Garden of Eden, condemned Adam to work to get what he needed to live, condemned Eve to give birth in pain, and placed cherubim to guard the entrance so that Adam and Eve would never eat from the "Tree of Life."

<u>God's Pet Peeve</u>: God hates haughty eyes. Provisions were in the Garden of Eden for them. They lived in paradise where they experienced no opposition and therefore had no understanding of joy or sorrow, pleasure, or pain. While in the Garden of Eden, Adam and Eve lived in God's presence.

<u>Jehovah's Compound Name</u>: Jehovah Jireh the Provider!

<u>Moral and Ethical</u>: They should have known that God already knew where they were and what state

they were in (they had failed). They were typically like a storm, not the kind you chase. "Today thou shalt be in paradise." Some rise by sin, and some virtue fall. Thus, the fall of Adam and Eve can be considered a process by which God guides his children to be rational, moral, and responsible. Through this process of "Knowing yourself." Adam and Eve would become mature human beings accountable to God for their actions. They were warned against disobedience and the pursuit of forbidden knowledge. The fall of man created a separation between humans and God. The fall of Adam and Eve was foreseen by the Heavenly Father, a necessary step in the plan of life and a great blessing to all of us. "Let us make man..." A plan for our redemption was made in the beginning.

Here are a few Morals and Ethical Lessons from Adam and Eve:

1. Free Will and Choice: The case highlights the significance of free will, the consequences of free will, and the consequences of the choices individuals make. They were given the choice to obey or disobey, illustrating the responsibility that comes with freedom.
2. Consequences of Actions: It teaches that actions have consequences, both for

individuals and for humanity as a whole. Adam and Eve's disobedience resulted in their expulsion from the Garden of Eden and introduced sin and suffering into the world.

3. Trust and Obedience: The case emphasizes the importance of trust and obedience in one's relationship with a higher power. Adam and Eve's disobedience stemmed from the lack of trust in God's instructions.

4. Accountability: It underscores the idea that individuals are accountable for their actions. They were held accountable for their disobedience, facing consequences for their choice.

5. The Nature of Temptation: This case highlights the nature of temptation and the vulnerability of human beings to succumb to it. They were tempted by the serpent to disobey God's command, showcasing the allure and danger of temptation.

Overall, their case serves as a cautionary tale about the consequences of disobedience, the importance of trust and obedience, and the accountability individuals have for their actions. It also addresses fundamental questions about human nature, morality, and the relationship between humanity and the divine.

1 John 1:19 – "If we confess our sins, he is faithful and just to forgive us our sins and to cleanse us from all unrighteousness."

Prayer: Father God, I confess my sinful nature and longing after the things of the world. I have sinned against you in thought, word, and deed, by what I have done and by what I have left undone. I have not loved my neighbors like myself. Guide me, O Lord, along the right path all the days of my life. For the sake of Your Son, Jesus Christ, have mercy on me. Forgive me, renew me, and lead me, so that I may delight in Your will and walk in Your ways to the glory of Your holy name, In Jesus' name, Amen.

No Matter How
Committed
Sin Will Be Exposed!

CASE # 2 – Conscience (In Secret) - Cain & Abel

- The sinful nature is all about self, pleasing self, promoting self, and preserving self, SIN is selfish.
- Fear the sins that you commit in secret because the witness of those sins is the judge's HIMSELF.
- An evil conscience is perpetually conscious of sin and failure and typically expects punishment. It is a conscience that is under condemnation.

Case #2: Cain & Abel

KINGDOM OF GOD COURT

The Offering	District of	Tilling the Field
Kingdom of God	vs	Judgement in a Criminal Case
Cain		#2

Title & Section	Nature of Offense	Count
Gen 4:1-18	Murder	1

CASE DOCKET #2 – In Secret: Cain and Abel

Fear the sins you have committed in secret because the witness of those sins is to judge Himself. Secret faults are sins we commit that we don't see or recognize as sins. Nevertheless, we are held accountable for our actions.

Guilty

<u>Text</u>: Genesis 4:1-18

<u>The LAW (the written Word)</u>: Thou shalt not kill (Exodus 20:13)

<u>Sin</u>: Murder
Because of our new Christian mindset, sin does not have the control over us that it once had. Yes, our hearts are naturally prone to sin, but with the power of the Holy Spirit, we can overcome sin and resist temptation. Do not let sin control the way you live; do not give in to sinful desires. Do not let any part of your body become an instrument of evil to serve sin. Instead, give yourselves completely to God, for you were dead, but now you have a new life. Use your whole body as an instrument to do what is right for the glory of God. Sin is no longer your master, for you no longer live under the requirements of the law. Instead, you live under the freedom of God's grace. Romans 6:12-14 NLT

<u>How Sin Was Committed</u>: The core moral behind Cain's actions in killing Abel is often interpreted as jealousy, resentment, and the consequence of unchecked anger. It highlights the destructive power of envy and the importance of controlling one's emotions to avoid committing acts of violence.

16

How Sin Was Exposed: In the biblical narrative, Cain's sin of killing his brother Abel was exposed when God confronted him about Abel's whereabouts. After Cain had killed Abel, God asked him where his brother was. Cain responded with the famous line, "Am I my brother's keeper?" However, God already knew what had happened and Cain's attempt to hide his sin was futile.

Evidence: Abel's blood cried out to God.

Judgment: Consequences of secret sin suffering defeat, and separation from God's presence and power. Cain's judgment was two-fold. Firstly, he was cursed by God to be a wanderer on the earth, unable to settle and cultivate the land effectively. Secondly, he was marked by God, a symbolic sign to protect him from being killed by anyone seeking vengeance. This mark, often interpreted as the "mark of Cain," served as a form of divine protection.

God's Pet Peeves: Hands that shed innocent blood.

Jehovah Compound Name: Shammah, God is here. His presence is with us.

Moral and Ethical: To restrict the artist is a crime.
It is to murder germinating. Yes, Abel was to be his
brother's keeper. Soft words turn away wrath. We
are held accountable for our actions.

1. After being addressed by God for killing his
   brother Abel, Cain should have learned
   several moral and ethical lessons:
2. The Sanctity of Life: Cain should have
   learned to value and respect the sanctity of
   human life. The act of murder is a grave sin,
   violating the intrinsic worth and dignity of
   another person.
3. The Consequences of Anger and Jealousy:
   Cain's actions were driven by jealousy and
   anger. He should have recognized the
   destructive power of these emotions and the
   importance of controlling them rather than
   letting them lead to harmful actions.
4. Personal Responsibility: Cain should have
   understood the importance of taking
   responsibility for his actions. When God
   asked Cain where Abel was, Cain responded
   evasively, "Am I my brother's keeper?" This
   deflection showed a lack of accountability,
   which is crucial for moral integrity.
5. The Importance of Right Intentions: God's
   rejection of Cain's offering and acceptance of

Abel's offering highlighted the importance of the sincerity and quality of one's actions and offering highlighted the importance of the sincerity and quality of one's actions and offerings to God. Cain should have learned to approach his duties with genuine intention and effort.

6. Consequences of Sin: Cain's punishment, being cursed to wander the earth and suffer hardship illustrates that sinful actions have serious and far-reaching consequences. Understanding this could have led Cain to reflect on the gravity of his wrongdoing and its impact on his life and others.

7. The Need for Repentance and Forgiveness: Although Cain expressed concern about his punishment, there is no biblical record of him expressing true remorse or seeking forgiveness. He should have learned the value of repentance and seeking reconciliation with God and others.

8. Brotherhood and Community Responsibility: Cain's rhetorical question, "Am I my brother's keeper?" should have led him to realize that individuals have a responsibility toward their family and community. Caring for others and ensuring their well-being is a fundamental ethical duty.

These lessons highlight the importance of empathy, self-control, accountability, and the recognition of the moral weight of one's actions. Cain's failure to learn these lessons serves as a cautionary tale about the dangers of allowing negative emotions to drive one's actions and the importance of moral reflection and growth.

Psalm 51:1-2, "Have mercy on me O God, according to Your steadfast love; according to Your abundant mercy blot out my transgressions. Wash me thoroughly from my iniquity, and cleanse me from my sin."

Prayer: Psalm 51:3-4, 7-10: "For I know my transgressions and my sin is ever before me. Against You, You only, have I sinned and done what is evil in Your sight, so that You may be justified in Your words and blameless in Your judgment. Purge me with hyssop, and I shall be clean; wash me, and I shall be whiter than snow. Let me hear joy and gladness; let the bones that You have broken rejoice. Hide Your face from my sins and blot out all my iniquities. Create in me a clean heart O, God, and renew a right spirit within me."

Lord, whatever I do in words or deeds let it be done in Jesus' name. Amen.

No Matter How Committed Sin Will Be Exposed!

**CASE # 3 - Under the Influence of
Drunkenness - Noah & Ham**

- Do not get drunk on wine, which leads to debauchery.
- Sin is an intrusion into a forbidden area - an overstepping of the divine boundary between good & evil. The Bible classifies us all as sinners and says that all are under sin.
- What was a sin and injustice also needs to be blessed with pardon, remorse, and reparation.

Case #3: Ham

KINGDOM OF GOD COURT

Honor	District of	After the Ark

Kingdom of God   vs   **Judgement in a Criminal Case**

Ham		#3

Title & Section	Nature of Offense	Count
Ex 20:2	Dishonor	1

CASE DOCKET #3 – Under the Influence: Ham

The heart is deceitful above all things, and desperately wicked: who can know it? I the LORD search the heart, I try the reins, even to give every man according to his ways and according to the fruit of his doings. Jeremiah 17:9-10

Text: Genesis 9:20-27

The LAW: (It is written) Honor thy Father (Exodus 20:12)
Proverbs 4:23 tells us to guard our hearts with diligence. This objective is achieved by filling our mind with God's Word regularly, proactively filtering what our mind consumes, and praying for wisdom and help from God (2 Peter 1:2 Philippians 4:6-7).

Sin: Dishonor to his Father (exposed his nakedness)
Although we will never be sinless or perfect in this present life, as Christians we are called to live in obedience to God. It's because we have the mindset of Christ, that we are fully equipped and capable of obeying. By his divine power, God has given us everything we need to live a godly life. We have received all of this by coming to know him, the one who called us to himself through his marvelous glory and excellence. 2 Peter 1:3 NLT

The Law emphasizes the importance of honoring one's parents, and it outlines both advantages and disadvantages associated with doing so.

Advantages of Honoring Thy Father (and Mother):
Long Life and Well-being:
- Exodus 20:12; "Honor your father and your mother, so that you may live long in the land the Lord your God is giving you."
- Deuteronomy 5:16: "Honor your father and your mother, as the Lord your God has commanded you, so that you may live long and that it may go well with you in the land the Lord your God is giving you."
- Ephesians 6:1-3: "Children, obey your parents in the Lord, for this is right. "Honor your father and mother, which is the first commandment with a promise- so that it may go well with you and that you may enjoy long life on earth."

Blessings and Prosperity:
- Proverbs 3:1-2: "My son, do not forget my teaching, but keep my commands in your heart, for they will prolong your life many years and bring you peace and prosperity."

- Proverbs 6:20-23: "My son, keep your father's command and do not forsake your mother's teaching. Bind them always on your heart: fasten them around your neck. When you walk, they will guide you; when you sleep, they will watch over you; when you awake, they are a light and will speak to you. For this command is a lamp, this teaching is a light, and correction and instruction are the way to life."

Disadvantages of Not Honoring Thy Father (and Mother):

- Punishment and Consequences:
- Deuteronomy 27:16: "Cursed is anyone who dishonors their father or mother." Then all the people shall say, "Amen!"
- Proverbs 20:20: "If someone curses their father or mother, their lamp will be snuffed out in pitch darkness."
- Proverbs 30:17: The eye that mocks a father, that scorns an aged mother, will be pecked out by the ravens of the valley, will be eaten by the vultures."

Disfavor and Misfortune:

- Matthew 15:4 "For God said, 'Honor your father and mother' and' Anyone who curses their father or mother is to be put to death."
- Ephesians 6:1-3 implies that not honoring parents results in missing out on the promised benefits of well-being and long life.

Overall, the Bible teaches that honoring one's parents brings about blessings, longevity, and severe consequences, including misfortune. These teachings underscore the value placed on familial respect and obedience within biblical ethics.

How Sin Was Committed: Noah became drunk after consuming wine from his vineyard and lay uncovered inside his tent. Ham, the father of Canaan, saw his father's nakedness and told his two brothers, Shem and Japheth, about it. Instead of covering his father respectfully, Ham chose to expose the situation. In contrast, Shem and Japheth took a garment, entered the tent backward so they would not see their father's nakedness, and covered him.

How Sin Was Exposed: Ham's sin of dishonoring his father, Noah, was exposed through his actions and the subsequent response of his brothers. The biblical account in Genesis 9:20-27 provides the details:

- Observation and Reporting: Ham saw his father Noah lying naked in his tent after becoming drunk. Instead of covering him, Ham went out and told his brothers, Shem and Japheth, about Noah's condition. This act of reporting rather than addressing the situation respectfully is viewed as dishonoring his father.
- Contrasting Actions of Shem and Japheth: Shem and Japheth responded differently. They took a garment, walked in backward so they would not see their father's nakedness, and covered him. This respectful and discrete action highlighted Ham's lack of respect and sensitivity.

Evidence: Noah drank too much wine. This incident serves as a cautionary tale about the dangers of drunkenness, the importance of self-control, and the significance of honoring and respecting family members, even in their moments of weakness.

Judgment: When Noah awoke and learned what had happened, he understood the dishonor Ham had brought upon him. Noah then pronounced a curse on Canaan, Ham's son, which revealed the gravity of Ham's offense. Noah's curse was, "Cursed be Canaan; a servant of servants shall he be to his brothers." (Genesis 9:25). This curse highlighted the seriousness of Ham's disrespectful behavior. He also blessed Shem and Japheth for their respectful actions. The exact nature of Ham's dishonor is subject to various interpretations, but it generally implies a lack of respect and an inappropriate response to his father's vulnerability.

In summary, Ham's sin was exposed through his inappropriate reaction to his father's vulnerability and the contrasting respectful actions of his brothers. Noah's awareness and subsequent curse on Canaan further revealed and condemned Ham's dishonor.

God's Pet Peeve: Feet that are quick to rush to evil.

Jehovah Compound Names: Shalom: Peace & Elohim: Covenant

Moral and Ethical: Ham should have learned several moral and ethical lessons from his actions and the consequences that followed:

Respect for Parental Authority: Ham should have understood the importance of respecting his father, Noah, even in a vulnerable state. Honoring one's parents is a fundamental ethical principle that he violated.

Respect for Privacy and Dignity: Ham's actions showed a disregard for his father's privacy and dignity. He should have learned to respect the personal boundaries and dignity of others, especially family members.

Appropriate Response to Vulnerable: Shem and Japheth's actions demonstrated the appropriate, respectful response.

The Importance of Discretion: Ham's decision to tell his brothers about Noah's condition rather than addressing it discreetly was a failure in discretion. He should have learned the value of handling sensitive situations with care and confidentiality.

Empathy and Compassion: Ham lacked empathy and compassion in dealing with his father's situation. He should have learned to be more empathetic and considerate of others' circumstances and feelings.

Consequences of Actions: Ham's actions had significant consequences, not just for him but for his descendants, He should have learned that irresponsible and disrespectful behavior can have long-lasting negative impacts.

Family Loyalty and Responsibility: Ham should have recognized the importance of family loyalty and the responsibility to support and protect family members, rather than brimming shame or harm to them.

These lessons emphasize the importance of respect, discretion, empathy, and understanding the broader impact of one's actions on others, particularly within the family context.

Psalm 19:14, "Let the words of my mouth and the meditation of my heart be acceptable in your sight, O Lord, my rock and my redeemer."

Prayer: Almighty God, I come boldly to Your throne for grace and mercy. I must admit, I cannot even discern the errors in my thoughts or ungodly intentions of my heart. But you see my inward being. Only You can see the truth in my secret heart. Cleanse me from any faults that I cannot see because You are a forgiving God, I confess and repent of those sins that I have intentionally committed. Free me from anything in my life that hinders my walk with You. Restore to me the joy of Your salvation in the name of Jesus Christ. Amen.

No Matter How Committed Sin Will Be Exposed!

**CASE # 4 - Years Before Discovery –
Joesph's Brothers**

- Of the seven deadly sins, envy is the silliest, because if you have it, you do not feel better. You feel worse. I have had some good times with gluttony. We would not get lust.
- All sin tends to be addictive, and the terminal point of addiction is what is called.
- Sin is a queer thing. It is not the breaking of divine commandments. It is the breaking of one's integrity.
- Many are saved from sin by being so inept at it.

Case #4: Joseph's Brothers

KINGDOM OF GOD COURT

The Coat of Many Colors		District of	Egypt

Kingdom of God	vs	Judgement in a Criminal Case

Joseph's Brothers	#4

Title & Section	Nature of Offense	Count
Ex 20:13	Attempted Murder	1
Ex 21:16	Kidnapping	1
Gen Ch 37-50	Human Trafficking	1
Prov 6:16-17	Lying	1

CASE DOCKET #4 – Years Before Discovery: Joseph's Brothers

Pain doesn't just show up in our lives for no reason. It's a sign that something in our lives needs to change. If we claim we have no sin, we are only fooling ourselves and not living in the truth. But if we confess our sins to him, he is faithful and just to forgive our sins and cleanse us from all wickedness. If we claim we have not sinned, we are calling God a liar and showing that his word has no place in our hearts. 1 John 1:8-10 NLT

<u>Text</u>: Genesis 37 Chapters
Joseph's brothers
At the beginning of Joseph's life seemed ideal. However, his life would quickly turn tragic. Through it all, Joseph remained faithful to God, and God never abandoned him. Also, God gave Joseph the supernatural ability to interpret dreams.

<u>The LAW</u>: (It is written) – Thou shall not lie. Honor thy father.

<u>Sin</u>: Anger, Jealousy, & Hatred
Jacob's showing favoritism to one brother caused strife among the brothers. Joseph, the most beloved of Jacob's sons, is hated by his envious brothers. Angry and jealous of Jacob's gift to Joseph, a resplendent "coat of many colors," the

brothers seize him and sell him to a party of Ishmaelites, or Midianites, who carry him to Egypt.

- Anger - "Be not quick in your spirit to become angry for anger lodges in the heart of fools".
- Jealousy - A Christian counselor suggests that people should humble themselves and ask God to reveal their motivations and feelings.
- Hatred - This leads to future anxiety, restlessness, obsessive thinking, and paranoia, which affects overall mental health. Even if you abhor something, it gives you a feeling of complete hatred.

How Sin Was Committed: In this case Joseph and his brother, which is found in the Book of Genesis (chapters 37-50). This is the list of sins and crimes that were committed by Joseph's brothers. These included: (These are the works of the flesh according to Galatians 5:19-21).

Envy and Hatred: Joseph's brothers were envious of him because their father, Jacob loved Joseph more and gave him a special coat (Genesis 37:3-4). This envy led to deep hatred.
Conspiracy and Plotting Harm: Motivated by jealousy, the brothers conspired to harm Joseph.

Initially, they plotted to kill him but later decided to throw him into the pit (Genesis 37:18-20).

Attempted Murder: The original plan was to kill Joseph and then lie about it to their father. This intention, even though not carried out, constituted the serious sin of contemplating murder (Genesis 37:18-20).

Kidnapping: Instead of killing Joseph, the brothers seized him and threw him into an empty cistern, effectively kidnapping him (Genesis 37:23-24). *Human Trafficking:* The brothers sold Joseph to a group of Ishmaelite traders for twenty pieces of silver. This act of selling their brother into slavery is a grave crime and sin (Genesis 37:26-28).

Deception and Lying: To cover up their actions, the brothers deceived their father, Jacob, by dipping Joseph's coat in goat's blood and presenting it to him, leading him to believe that Joseph had been killed by a wild animal (Genesis 37:31-33).

Lack of Compassion and Responsibility: The brothers showed a severe lack of compassion for Joseph and a complete disregard for their responsibility to protect and care for their siblings.

How Sin Was Exposed: After being incarcerated and correctly interpreting the dreams of Pharaoh, Joseph rises to second-in-command in Egypt and saves Egypt during a famine. He waited on God for 13 years before he saw the manifestation of the promise (From the birth of his dreams to their final fulfillment. The fulfillment took 22 years). Not only did he have to wait, but he also went through hell while he waited. Sold into slavery by his envious brothers and then accused of rape and sent to prison, Joseph had a tough time. It took years before the truth was discovered because Joseph was sold into slavery and eventually rose to a position of power in Egypt while his brothers remained in Canaan. The discovery came when Joseph's brothers traveled to Egypt seeking food during a famine and encountered Joseph, who became a high-ranking official in the Egyptian government.

Evidence: Joseph identified his brothers. We can hypothesize that Joseph's weeping was because of his unique situation, not his unique personality. It images during the reunion with his family when Joseph cannot or will not reveal his identity until the time is right (God's timing). Joseph is discovered to be alive.

<u>Judgment</u>: When we don't understand why we are
subjected to hardships, trials, grief, and
deprivation of many kinds that's found in the case
when Joseph finally revealed his identity to his
brothers. "God sent me ahead of you to preserve
for you a remnant on earth and to save your lives
by a great deliverance. So then, it was not you who
sent me here, but God" (Gen. 45: 7-8).
What a perspective Joseph had on his role in this
God-given case! He tells his brothers not to keep
torturing themselves with regrets about their
treachery toward him. It all happened to fulfill the
plan and purpose of God to protect the Christ line
by providing for his covenant people. Joseph
carried the spirit of wisdom, understanding the
perfection of God's sovereign grace. Citing his
garment was eventually cleared. Potiphar's wife
responds, "Truly I have sinned and wronged him.
Now don't be upset, for I will appease him, and he
will honor you more than all of your friends, and
he will make you a great man and a ruler over all
the freemen and nobles of Pharaoh." Potiphar's
wife petitions Joseph and begs his forgiveness.
Potiphar's wife is condemned to suffer a burning
fever for all eternity. Joseph patiently endured
great suffering and loss in the end and declared a
shining supernatural perspective on all that had
transpired in his eventual life.

Guilty

<u>God's Pet Peeve</u>: A lying tongue and a heart that
devises wicked schemes.

<u>Jehovah Compound Name</u>: Nissi - Victory! The
Lord our banner!

<u>Moral and Ethical</u>: These actions reflect a series of
moral failings and grave sins, including envy,
hatred, conspiracy to commit murder, kidnapping,
human trafficking, and deception.
This case of Joseph and his brothers ultimately
serves as a powerful narrative about the
consequences of sin and the possibilities of
forgiveness and redemption.

James 4:8-10, "Draw near to God, and he will draw
near to you. Cleanse your hands, you sinner, and
purify your hearts, you double-minded. Be
wretched and mourn and weep. Let your laughter
be turned to mourning and your joy to gloom.
Humble yourselves before the Lord, and he will
exalt you."

Prayer: Lord, what is man that thou are mindful of
him? Lord God, what hope You give me in those
words in James 4:8-10, I long to draw near to you,
but my unconfessed sin stands in the way. I

confess my sins to you right now and repent with sorrow. Bring a fresh awareness of the seriousness of my sin and how it separates me from You. My sin has caused that distance and I confess it now. I pray that your mighty name be exalted in my life. Thank you for drawing near to me when I continuously pull away from You. Grant me these requests in Jesus' name. Amen

No Matter How Committed Sin Will Be Exposed!

CASE # 5 - Well Covered UP - Achan

- There is no original sin, it has all been done before.
- The Bible says that whosoever breaks one law is guilty of breaking all of them.
- Sin is the transgression of the law of God.
- Sin has many tools, but a lie is the handle that fits them all

Case #5: Achan

KINGDOM OF GOD COURT

The Spoils	District of	Battle of Ai

Kingdom of God	vs	Judgement in a Criminal Case

Achan		#5

Title & Section	Nature of Offense	Count
Ex 20:17	Covetousness	1
Ex 20:15	Stealing	3

CASE DOCKET #5 - Well Covered Up: Achan

The gold and silver Achan stole were stolen from God Himself. The precious metals were to be added to the treasury of the Lord, and in stealing them Achan robbed God directly. Achan's disobedience was also an insult to God's holiness and His command of His people.

Texts: Joshua 7 and Numbers 32:23

The LAW: (It is written) - Thou Shalt Not Covet. Thou shalt not steal. (Exodus 20:15,17) The Israelites were to take nothing from Jericho. Everything in it was 'accursed' or 'devoted to destruction.'

Sin: Covetousness led to stealing. God warned that anyone taking the spoils from Jericho would "make the camp of Israel to destruction and bring trouble on it" Joshua 6:18-19.

How Sin Was Committed: Achan violated the 8th and 9th commandments. He stole property that was not his and coveted items of his pagan neighbors. He has violated God's instructions in Deuteronomy 20:10-20; he lied. He stole treasure from Jericho and hid it for himself instead of giving it to the Lord. Achan, one man, sinned by stealing a garment, 200 shekels of silver, and a wedge of gold during the heat of battle after having been instructed that all the booty from Jericho was devoted to God. (Joshua 6:17-19; 7:1:20-23). He had no accomplices, and no one saw him do it.

Nevertheless, Israel's army became paralyzed with fear when they attacked the little city of Ai (verses 4-5). Joshua faltered and became confused (verses 6-9). Thirty-six more died, wives were widowed and children lost fathers.

How Sin Was Exposed: God revealed that a man from Zabdi's family was the one who had kept some of the riches of Jericho. The man's name was Achan. His sin was discovered of course (Numbers 32:23). God gave Achan a night to consider his sin and come to Him in repentance (Joshua 7:13). Achan does not avail himself of God's mercy and patience. One might say that the sin was atoned for when they found out what Achan had done. When God saw it, however, He analyzed the sin according to different standards. He was dealing with His people, and He wanted to make sure that a witness was made so that there would be information for those of the Church in the future.

Evidence: The garment and the gold and silver cup were found under the rug in Achan's tent. All the spoils of Jericho had to be dedicated to the Lord and burned with fire except for the gold and silver which was to be taken to the Tabernacle.

Judgment: What we see here is a clear beginning of 'the body' analogy that later becomes so important to the church in the New Testament. He shows us plainly that sin has a natural leavening effect. It increases; it will not just lie there and die.

Correction must be made to ensure that it does not spread affecting others. God commanded that Achan and his entire family and all his possessions be destroyed, a punishment that seems very harsh to us today. Achan's sin affected the entire nation of Israel. Further, his sin caused God's blessing upon the Israelites to be withheld in the battle against the city of Ai, thirty-six men who were not involved in Achan's sin died because of his sin.

Also, the gold and silver were stolen from God Himself. Achan caused Israel a lot of trouble. Now the LORD is paying him back with the same trouble he caused and stoned Achan to death and his family. The people of Israel made a fire and burned the bodies, including what he stole, and all his possessions.

God's Pet Peeve: Thou shall not steal. Achan disobeyed and took the spoils for himself, and the anger of the LORD was kindled against the children of Israel (Joshua 7:1). The nation as a whole was in a covenant relationship with God and when one member transgressed that covenant, the entire nation's relationship with Him was damaged. Achan's sin defiled the other members of the community as well as himself. A similar situation is seen in the sin of Adam and Eve and its effect on the whole of mankind.

Jehovah Compound Name: Jireh - Provider

Moral and Ethical: Achan had a strong pull on his allegiance. A greedy man brings trouble to his family. Achan hid the stuff. We must trust God for directions. If by chance we are defeated, we should not give up. We should ask ourselves why we failed. Then we need to turn to the Lord, correct the problem, and try again. God takes a personal interest in His people. Things happen out in the world, and He does nothing. But when things happen within His church, He is concerned for the well-being of His people, and He takes action.

2 Chronicles 7:14, "If my people who are called by my name humble themselves, and pray and seek my face and turn from their wicked ways, then I will hear from heaven and will forgive their sin and heal their land."

Prayer: Most Holy Lord, each day I am surrounded by the sins of the world and that includes pride. I have allowed pride to keep me from humbling myself before You. This world does not celebrate humbleness, but You honor it. Father, turn my face toward You. Cleanse me of pride and anything else that keeps me from seeking You. I pray that your good things continuously show me a better way to live a new life centered on You. In Jesus' name. Amen

No Matter How Committed Sin Will Be Exposed!

CASE #6 - Misusing God's Gift - Samson & Delilah

- Without the spice of guilt, sin cannot be fully savored.
- The mind sins, not the body, if there is no intention, there is no blame.
- One leak will sink a ship: one sin will destroy a sinner.
- Sin is whatever obscures the soul.
- That which we call sin in others is an experiment for us.

Case #6: Samson & Delilah

KINGDOM OF GOD COURT

Cutting the Anointing	District of	Philistine

Kingdom of God	vs	Judgement in a Criminal Case

Samson & Delilah		#6

Title & Section	Nature of Offense	Count
I Cor 10:14	Idolatry	1
Prov 16:5 & 16:18	Pride	1
Eph 4:11-12	Misuse of Gift	1

CASE DOCKET #6 - Misusing God's Gift: Samson & Delilah

Use God's gift wisely and for God's benefit. To do otherwise is to "waste our talents." Whatever we do in words or deeds, do it for the glory of God. Only what we will do for Christ will last. Samson was called by the Lord to help free the Israelites from the Philistines. Samson's mission would require physical strength. The Lord made a covenant with Samson that as long as he obeyed the Lord, he would be physically strong. Samson had lots of folly within himself. Samson loved the world. Samson desired to please himself and control his own life. He enjoyed spending time at parties with his enemies. His life shows his proud attitude controlled him. He thought nobody could overcome him, so, he used hard questions for fun (Judges 16:14-16). Then there is something even worse, he had awful spiritual pride. He came from a good home (his parents loved and obeyed God; he had an attractive nature (his name means 'sunlight'). There was no doubt that Samson was attractive. He could have been of great use to God. But his nature became dangerous to him. He loved to be popular. This ruined him in the end; He had a good religious tradition (Judges 13:3-5 and Numbers 6:2-8). He should have remembered them. He was responsible to God. Religious tradition is no good if we do not love or obey God. Although he had true experiences of the Holy Spirit's power in his life, he continued to be worldly. He even had experiences of answered prayers which should have encouraged him to stay close to God.

Text: Judges 16 Chapter

Idolatry - I Corinthian 10:14 "Wherefore, my dearly beloved, flee from idolatry."

Pride - Proverbs 16:5: "The Lord detests all the proud heart. Be sure of this: They will not go unpunished"

Pride - Proverbs 16:18- "Pride goes before destruction, a haughty spirit before a fall."

Misusing God's Gift - Eph 4:11-12 "...for the equipping of the saints for the work of ministry, for the edifying of the body of Christ."

The LAW: (It is written) He that exalts himself shall be brought abase, but he who humbles himself shall be exalted. Live by the vow never cut his hair or drink any alcohol.

Sin: Idolatry and Pride

How Sin Was Committed: Samson misused his divine gift. He used his power recklessly for personal benefit. The gift is not for selfish gains but to bless others. However, Samson used the power God had given him for his advantage. Because he knew God had given this special power not available to others, he kept on getting himself in trouble and using this power on each occasion to bail himself out. This could not have been the purpose for which God endowed.

You will see the same abuse of divine power in Judges 16:1-3. God never sent him to go into a harlot but when he was in trouble, it was the power of God that he abused to get out of the trouble.

Samson must have been deluded by the unprecedented power of God in his life to think that he could always get out of any situation no matter the type of life he lived.

How Sin Was Exposed: His worst flaw was he only called on God twice when he was in trouble. He should have had fellowship with God. He was secretive but had poor judgment about who to confide in. In the end, Samson realized his awful mistakes when he broke his covenant through unrighteous action. He made the wrong choice in lusting after Delilah who was loyal to the Philistine. Due to his lust for her, he forsook his faith. Delilah was cunning in discovering the source of his strength. After three failed attempts, she gets him to tell his secret. She took his confidence to betray him to his enemies. No one who sleeps on the lap of Delilah can survive her ambush. Samson should have run away from Delilah...just as Joseph ran away from Mrs. Potiphar.

Evidence: While he slept, the faithless Delilah brought in a Philistine who cut Samson's hair, draining his strength.
- His failures:
- He lacked a sense of divine destiny.
- He misused his divine gifts.
- He was temperamental and revengeful.
- He was lustful.
- He was secretive but had poor judgment on whom to confide in.
- He was tricky.
- He was callous and impulsive.
- He was disorderly or disorganized.
- He was proud.
- He had no fellowship with God.
- He never worked on his character flaws.

Judgment: Samson killed more people at his death than when he was alive; but it was because of the mercy of God, not because Samson was careful to live a holy life. God is a merciful God!

It is noteworthy that the New Testament does not mention any of the mistakes of Samson. Samson is rather mentioned alongside Gideon, Barak, David, Samuel, and the prophets- patriarchs of faith, **"who through faith subdued kingdoms, worked righteousness, obtained promises, stopped mouths of lions, quenched the violence of fire, escaped the edge of the sword, out of weakness were made strong, became valiant in battle, turned to fight the armies of the aliens."** **(Hebrews 11: 32-34).**

God's Pet Peeve: A proud look (the attitude that makes one overestimate oneself and discount others).

Jehovah Compound Name: Tsidkenu - Righteousness

Moral and Ethical: We Learn to give the glory to God. must beware of pride. Whatever great work God is doing through us, do not ascribe the success to ourselves.

Always remember to work on our character flaws. Samson never learned from his mistakes. For instance, look at how lust for women remained a problem in his life till he died. Nobody is perfect. All of us have made mistakes at one point or the other in our lives but God expects us to learn from our mistakes and change for the better.

God makes it clear that those who engage in any form of idolatry will have no part in HIS kingdom.

1. Beware of Temptation: Samson's downfall came through his relationship with Delilah, who tempted him and ultimately betrayed him. This teaches the importance of being cautious and aware of temptation in our lives.

2. Strength Alone is Not Enough: Despite Samson's incredible physical strength, he was still vulnerable to deceit and manipulation. This emphasizes the importance of character, wisdom, and discernment alongside any physical or material abilities.

3. The Consequence of Pride: Samson's pride and arrogance led him to make rash decisions, such as revealing the source of his strength to Delilah. This serves as a warning against the dangers of hubris and overestimating one's abilities.

4. The Power of Repentance: Despite his mistakes, Samson ultimately repented and turned back to God. This highlights the importance of acknowledging our faults,

seeking forgiveness, and striving to make amends.

5. The Impact of Choices on Others: Delilah's actions not only affected Samson but also had consequences for the entire nation of Israel. This underscores the interconnectedness of our choices and the potential ripple effects they can have on others.

6. The Role of Faithfulness: Samson's faithfulness to God wavered throughout his case, but ultimately, he demonstrated faith in God's plan for him, even in his darkest moments. This illustrates the importance of remaining faithful and trusting in a higher power, even when challenges and trials.

These lessons from the case of Samson and Delilah can serve as valuable guides for navigating our own moral and ethical dilemmas in life.

Matthew 6:9-13, "Our Father in heaven, hallowed be Your name, your kingdom come, your will be done, on earth as it is in heaven. Give us this day our daily bread, and forgive us our debts, as we also have forgiven our debtors. And lead us not into temptation but deliver us from evil."

Prayer: Our Father which art, you are the God of my salvation. The prayer you taught your disciples demonstrated how You long for us to live free from guilt, sin, and unforgiveness. I confess my sins to you now, Father. Give me the tenacity and strength to mourn over and repent of my sin to turn my heart toward You continuously. Thank you for caring for your prodigal sons in Jesus' name. Amen

No Matter How
Committed
Sin Will Be Exposed!

CASE # 7 - In A Moment of an Impulse - David & Bathsheba

- I believe no man has ever scolded out his sin.
- Confession, you see, is not a punishment for sin, it is an isolation of sin so it can be exposed and extracted.
- Repentance is more than just being sorry for our sins. It is a complete turning away from our total depravity.
- We are not punished for our sins but by them.
- Fashion in sin change.
- The most dangerous thing you can do is to take any one impulse of your nature and set it up as the thing you ought to follow at all costs. All these primary impulses, not easily described in words, are the springs of man's actions.

Case #7: David & Bathsheba

KINGDOM OF GOD COURT

Wartime		District of	Jerusalem

Kingdom of God	vs	Judgement in a Criminal Case

David & Bathsheba		#7

Title & Section	Nature of Offense	Count
Ex 20:17	Covetousness	1
Ex 20:14	Adultery	1
Ex 20:13	Murder	1

CASE DOCKET #7 - Moment of Impulse - David and Bathsheba

Although we all may have our individual "heart struggles" to guard against, I believe all of them essentially fall into one of four main categories according to Scripture: sin, lies, deception, and idols. We need to embrace the concepts of sin. God is the one who defines sin, not us. Sin is any and everything that doesn't meet God's Holy Standards as established by His righteousness. And the Bible is clear on what things fall into the sin category. Anytime we start to question doubt, compromise, or subtract from what God calls sin, that should ALWAYS be a **WARNING SIGN TO US!!!** In other words, if you find yourself always looking for a way to defend your sin, make excuses for it, or call it something else other than sin, that should be cause for concern. Consequently, impulse has several thorns in our flesh. For instance:

Spontaneous Action: often leads to immediate actions without thought of contemplation or planning. This can result in decisions made hastily or without fail, and awareness of potential outcomes.

Emotional Influence: is frequently driven by emotions, such as anger, desire, or excitement. These strong feelings can override rational thinking and lead to impulsive behavior.

Risk Factors: impulse actions may carry significant risk, as often undertaken without weighing the potential consequences. This can lead to regrettable outcomes of harm to oneself or others.

Lack of Control: individuals experiencing impulses feel a sense of loss of control over their actions. This can contribute to feelings of guilt or shame afterward, especially if the actions result in negative consequences.

Temporal Perspective: impulse provides immediate gratification over long-term considerations. This can lead to decisions that provide temporary satisfaction but may be detrimental in the long run.

Cognition Biases: various cognitive biases such as an anchoring or availability bias, can influence impulse decision-making by skewing perceptions and judgments.

Text: Ex 20:13-14, 17, 2 Sam 12:1-15

The LAW: (It is written) - Thou shalt not commit adultery & Thou shalt Not Kill. Thou shalt not covet (Exodus 20:13-14, 17)
An impulse person has a short fuse and can ruin everything, but the wise show self-control. Impulse refers to a sudden involuntary inclination or urge to act. It often occurs without much forethought or consequences that are driven by desire, leading to grave consequences both personally and politically.

Sin: Lust, Adultery & Murder

<u>How Sin Was Committed</u>: God chose to remove Israel's first king Saul and appoint David as king. Even knowing all the sins David would commit, God referred to him as "a man after his own heart": And when He had removed him, He raised David to be their king: of him He testified and said, "I have found David the son of Jesse, a man after My own heart [conforming to My will and purposes], who will do all My will." (Acts 13:22 AMP) To summarize David's case, he had many victories as King of Israel. But David fell into sin. He lusted after a married woman named Bathsheba and slept with her, then got her pregnant. To cover up his sin, David arranged for Bathsheba's husband to be placed in a vulnerable position in battle, resulting in his death.

Here is a detailed look at King David's actions involving Bathsheba and the resulting consequences:

David's Actions: Lust and Adultery, Deception, Murder, Marrying Bathsheba, and Taking Bathsheba as Wife

Seeing Bathsheba: While on the roof of his place, King David saw Bathsheba bathing. He found her very beautiful and desired her.

Summoning Bathsheba: David sent messages to bring Bathsheba to him. Despite knowing she was married to Uriah the Hittite, one of his loyal soldiers, David slept with her, leading to her pregnancy (2 Samuel 11:2-5).

Calling Uriah Home: To conceal the adultery, David called Uriah back from the battlefield, hoping he would sleep with his wife Bathsheba and think the child was his own.

Uriah's Integrity: Uriah, out of loyalty to his fellow soldiers, refused to go home and sleep with his wife while the Ark of the Covenant and his comrades were in battle. He stayed at the palace entrance instead (2 Samuel 11:6-13).

Arranging Uriah's Death: When his initial plan failed, David wrote a letter to Joab, the commander of the army, instructing him to place Uriah at the front of the fiercest battle and then withdraw support so that Uriah would be killed.

Uriah's Death: Joab followed David's instructions, and Uriah was killed in battle (2 Samuel 11:14-17). After Uriah's death, David brought Bathsheba to his house, and she became his wife and bore him a son (2 Samuel 11:26-27).

How Sin Was Exposed: David then befriended her husband Urian (one of his soldiers) Then he put a plan in place to have him killed in battle. His plan succeeded and Uriah was reported dead. Bathsheba mourned briefly, and then David married her to cover up the affair, and they continued with day-to-day life as if nothing ever happened. This event is often cited as an example of the consequences of succumbing to impulse and the abuse of power. Despite David's attention to conceal his wrongdoing, God sent his servant Nathan to confront David regarding the situation and to pronounce the punishment He had set forth. Then Nathan said to David, "You are that man! The Lord, the God of Israel, says: I anointed you king of Israel and saved you from the power of Saul. I gave you your master's house and his wives and the kingdoms of Israel and Judah. And if that had not been enough, I would have given you much, much more. Why, then, have you despised the word of the Lord and done this horrible deed? For you have murdered Uriah the Hittite with the sword of the Ammonites and stolen his wife."

Evidence:
Bathsheba was pregnant while her husband was off to war, and a plot was planned for her husband to be killed.

<u>Judgment</u>: Nathan confronted David about his sin found in 2 Samuel 12:15.

In one of the darkest hours of his life, King David committed adultery with Bathsheba and then had her husband, Uriah killed. God sent the prophet Nathan to tell David a parable of a rich man who passed over his flock and took a poor man's lamb to feed his guest. The parable aroused David's anger at the injustice of all until Nathan says, in a dramatic moment, "Thou art the man." Realizing the enormity of his sin, David expressed his repentance in Psalm 51.

And David said unto Nathan, I have sinned against the Lord. And Nathan said unto David, The Lord also hath put away thy sin; thou hath put away thy sin; thou shalt not die. Howbeit, because by thy deed thou hath given great occasion to the enemies of the Lord to blaspheme, the child also that is born unto thee shall surely die. And Nathan departed unto his house. And the Lord struck the child that Uriah's wife bared unto David, and it was very sick.

<u>Divine Judgment</u>: Repentance upon realizing the severity of his sins, David repented and sought

forgiveness from God. The remainder of this case reveals the rest of David's life. Although David is forgiven, he still bears the exact consequences of his sin as determined by God through Nathan. The child that David and Bathsheba had died.

- Confrontation by Nathan: The prophet Nathan confronted David, telling him a parable about a rich man who stole a poor man's lamb. When David condemned the man in the story, Nathan revealed that David was that man. Nathan declared God's judgment upon David, saying that the sword would never depart from his house (2 Samuel 12:1-12).
- Death of the Child (Illness and Death): The child born to David and Bathsheba became severely ill and died despite David's prayers and fasting (2 Samuel 12:15-18).
- Continued Family Strife: Turmoil in David's House: As a result of David's sin, his family faced ongoing conflict and tragedy. His son Amnon raped his half-sister Tamar, leading to Tamar's brother Absalom killing Amnon in revenge (2 Samuel 13).
- Rebellion of Absalom: Absalom eventually led a rebellion against David, causing a civil war.

Absalom was later killed in battle, adding to David's grief (2 Samuel 12:15-18).

- Personal Remorse (David's Repentance): David expressed deep remorse for his sins in Psalms, especially in Psalm 51, where he pleaded for God's mercy and forgiveness.

God's Pet Peeve: "A heart that devises wicked schemes (plan)," 12:7-12 NLT
Forgiveness NEVER excludes us from God's discipline as His children. There are times when God will punish and there are times when he will show mercy and we can never demand either. Hence, we can never say God is unfair. For God said to Moses, "I will show compassion to anyone I choose." It is God who decides to show mercy. We can neither choose it nor work for it. (Romans 9:14-16 NLT)

Jehovah Compound Name: Elohim - Covenant

Moral and Ethical: To thy own self be true! After this confrontation, there is no denial, no excuses, no lying, and no running away. David a man after God's own heart simply responds as follows: Then David confessed to Nathan, "I have sinned against the Lord." (1 Samuel 12:13a NLT) His response is simple and genuine. In his confession, David agrees with God by acknowledging his sin, setting forth a great example of what it means to live as a child of God, truly "a man after God's own heart." When we fall, we often react the way David initially did; we ignore, hide, manipulate, pretend it didn't happen, and go on with life. Oftentimes, we don't acknowledge that we have sinned against the Lord until we too, are confronted. Regardless of how we sin, like David, we must always acknowledge that sin is sin. We MUST learn to agree with God. We can never say that something is NOT a sin that God has already deemed as sin in His Word, whether it's lying, cheating, adultery, fornication, stealing, homosexuality, jealousy, pride, or gossiping. Agreeing with God about what sin is doesn't mean we will never sin again. It means that when we do sin, we will acknowledge it as such by confessing it to God and any other involved parties and doing whatever is necessary to make things right if possible. The beauty of acknowledging and agreeing with God is when we sin, He forgives us.

The moral and ethical lessons to be learned from this case consist of:

- Consequences of Lust and Temptation: David's affair with Bathsheba and subsequent actions illustrate the consequences of yielding to lust and temptation. It serves as a cautionary tale about the destructive power of unchecked desires.

- Abuse of Power: Our ministry is never to be used as a weapon; only as a tool for the upbuilding of God's kingdom. As a king, David abused his authority by sleeping with Bathsheba. His sin highlights the misuse of power and leaders' responsibility to act justly and ethically.

- Responsibility for Actions: David's attempt to cover up his sin by arranging for Uriah's death demonstrates the lengths individuals may go to avoid taking responsibility for their actions. The case emphasizes the importance of accountability for one's choices.

- Repentance and Forgiveness: After being confronted by the prophet Nathan, David, repented. His case illustrates the possibility of redemption through genuine remorse and seeking forgiveness from God.

- Impact on Others: The ripple effects of David's sin extended beyond himself and Bathsheba to include Uriah, Bathsheba's husband, and the community. The case underscores how personal decisions can have consequences for others.

God's Justice and Mercy: Despite David's wrongdoing the data reflects God's justice and mercy. While David faced consequences for his actions, God remained faithful and offered forgiveness upon repentance.

Overall, King David's actions of lusting after Bathsheba, committing adultery, and orchestrating Uriah's murder led to severe personal and family consequences, and the immediate result was the death of his and Bathsheba's child. The long-term effect, his household was plagued by violence, betrayal, and rebellion. Despite these consequences, David sought repentance and was forgiven by God, though he still faced the repercussions of his actions. The case of David and Bathsheba serves as a reminder of the complexities of human nature, the importance of ethical conduct, and the possibility of redemption even in the face of grave wrongdoing.

Be sure your sin will find you out...

Joel 2:12, "Yet even now," declares the Lord, "return to me with all your heart, with fasting, with weeping, and with mourning."

Prayer: Lord God, you know all things, and nothing is hidden from you...I confess that I have put my agenda ahead of yours. I have trusted my timing instead of yours. I have trusted my cleverness rather than leaned into your holiness. And have not lived in a way that shows the glory of God in my life. Purify my heart, Lord. I ask for your forgiveness. Set my feet on the right path that leads to the kingdom of heaven and intimacy with you in Jesus' name. Amen

No Matter How Committed Sin Will Be Exposed!

CASE # 8 - Plotted by Others - Ahab & Jezebel

- Every uncorrected error and unrepented sin is, in its own right, a fountain of fresh error and fresh sin flowing into the end of time.
- To sin is to state, "God, I do not want you to be my king. I prefer a kingless kingdom, or better still, a kingdom in which I am King."
- Sin looks much more terrible to those who look at it than to those who do it.
- Sin arrived as a passerby. Next, it lingered for a moment. Then, it came as a visitor and finally became master of the house.

Case #8: Ahab & Jezebel

KINGDOM OF GOD COURT

Naboth's Vineyard	District of	Jezreel

Kingdom of God	vs	Judgement in a Criminal Case

Ahab & Jezebel		#8

Title & Section	Nature of Offense	Count
Prov 6:7	Lying	1
Ex 20:13	Accessory to Murder	1
Ex 20:17	Coveted	1

CASE DOCKET #8 - Plotted - Ahab and His Wife Jezebel

Woe to those who plan inquiry, to those who plot evil on their beds! Whoever digs a pit will fall into it, if someone rolls a stone, it will roll back on them. Naboth owned a vineyard that was close to

Ahab's place in Jezreel. Ahab asked Naboth if he could buy the vineyard so that he could use it as a vegetable (or herb) garden. Naboth refused because the land was his ancestral inheritance. He was an innocent man who suffered unjustly at the hands of King Ahab and his wife Jezebel.

Text: 1 Kings 21:1-16

The LAW: (It is written) - Thou shalt not covet. Thou shalt not bear false witness against thy neighbor." "A good man leaves an inheritance to his children's children." Proverbs 13:22

Sin: Lied and plotted an evil false witness against their neighbor (Naboth). Ahab's sin led the whole nation to sin against God.

How Sin Was Committed: Jezebel plotted the death of Naboth to help her husband get the vineyard he wanted in Jezreel. She deceitfully accused Naboth, the owner of the vineyard, of blasphemy which resulted in his execution.

How Sin Was Exposed: Nevertheless, their sin was exposed and condemned by the prophet Elijah, who delivered a message from God denouncing their actions and prophesying punishment for their descendants. 2 Kings 9:30-37, after Jezebel's death, her body was thrown out the window, and it was left on the street. Dogs came and ate her flesh, fulfilling the prophecy made against her by Elijah.

Evidence: Naboth, from his stance, had no option but to refuse the king's offer. He did not hesitate or blink in his refusal to the king. For him, the matter is unambiguous, even if the king cannot fathom such refusal. Naboth refused to give up the inheritance of his father. Ahab was powerless before this peasant's refusal and could only fall into depression. Hence, Ahab's wife took revenge into her hands. She was determined Ahab would secure the vineyard.

Judgment: Death came to both of them, Ahab and his wife. Death was passed down to their offspring as well. Ahab was king of Israel, and his wife Jezebel was known for promoting idol worship and leading Israel away from the true God. This prophecy was fulfilled when Ahab died in battle, and his body was left on the battlefield to be eaten by dogs, just as Elijah had foretold. As for Jezebel, her fate was equally grim. She was thrown out of the window by her servants at the command of Jehu, a military commander who became king after overthrowing Ahab's throne. Jezebel's body was left on the street to be eaten by dogs, fulfilling another prophecy concerning her fate. The judgment upon Ahab and Jezebel serves as a sobering reminder of the consequences of leading others astray and defying God's commands. It underscores the principle of divine justice and the accountability of individuals, even those in positions of power and authority.

God's Pet Peeve:
1. Feet that are quick to rush into evil
2. A false witness who lies
3. A man who stirs up dissension among the brothers.

Jehovah Compound Names: Jireh – Provider, Shammah - Presence of God

Moral and Ethical:
1. Respect for Property Rights: Naboth's refusal to sell his ancestral inheritance highlights the importance of respecting property rights and honoring family legacies.
2. The Dangers of Greed and Covetousness: Ahab's desire for Naboth's vineyard led him to abandon ethical principles and engage in deceitful and unjust actions to satisfy his desire.

3. Consequences of Dishonesty and Injustice: Ahab and Jezebel's plot against Naboth ultimately led to their downfall, demonstrating that dishonesty and injustice have severe consequences.
4. Accountability to God: The case emphasizes that individuals are ultimately accountable, and even kings are subject to divine judgment.
5. The Role of Prophets and Moral Courage: Elijah's condemnation of Ahab and Jezebel's actions highlights the importance of prophets and individuals who have the moral courage to speak out against injustice and hold leaders accountable.

Overall, the case underscores the importance of integrity, respect for others, and accountability for personal and political conduct.

2 Peter 3:9, "The Lord is not slow to fulfill his promise as some count slowness, but is patient toward you, not wishing that any should perish, but that all should reach repentance."

Prayer: Mighty God, Father of creation…you control everything. All flesh is in the palms of your hands. You could condemn the entire world, including me, at this very moment. Yet You want us to live eternally with you rather than perish in our sin. Father, I repent of my sins whether I know about them or am blind to them. Repentance is painful, but my sorrow is a gift of your grace that draws me closer to you. Thank you for loving me so much. Lord, you know my heart Grant me forgiveness in Jesus' name. Amen

No Matter How Committed Sin Will Be Exposed!

CASE # 9 - Approval of Authority - Herod & Herodias

- Sin is not making bad choices or mistakes. Sin is having the desire in our hearts to do the will of the enemy of God.
- Sin is not just breaking the rules; it is putting yourself in the place of God as savior, Lord, and judge just as each son sought to displace the authority of the father in his own life.

Case #9: Herod & Herodias

KINGDOM OF GOD COURT

Dancing Dangers	District of	King Herod's Court

Kingdom of God	vs	Judgement in a Criminal Case

Herod & Herodias		#9

Title & Section	Nature of Offense	Count
Deu 27:25	Murder	1

CASE DOCKET #9 – Approval of Authority – Herod & Herodias

Difference between authority and power: Power is an entity or individual's ability to control or direct others, while authority is influence that is predicated on perceived legitimacy. The reality is that humans are sinful. And sinful beings use authority sinfully. They usually sin through means of sin of attitude, action, neglect, and intent. The classification of sin into these four categories is a common framework used in moral and religious teachings. Here's a brief overview of each type:

1. Sins of Attitude: These sins involve wrongful attitudes or thoughts, such as envy, pride, greed, lust, and hatred. While these sins may not always manifest in outward actions, they are considered morally significant because they reflect the state of one's heart and character.

2. Action: These sins involve wrong actions or behaviors that transgress moral or ethical principles. Examples include lying, stealing, cheating, adultery, murder, and various forms of violence. Sins of action are often more readily observable and may have direct consequences for oneself and others.

3. Sins of Neglect: These sins involve failing to do what is right or failing to fulfill one's moral obligations. This could include neglecting to help those in need, failing to speak up against injustice, or neglecting one's duties and responsibilities.

<u>Text</u>: Matthew 14:3-5; Mark 6:17-20, Prov 17:15

<u>The LAW</u>: (It is written) - Be Ye Holy! God alone is the ultimate authority. Matthew 6:13

<u>Sin</u>: Murder

<u>How Sin Was Committed</u>: Herod sent men to arrest John, bound him, and put him in prison on account of Herodias, his brother Philip's wife because Herod had married her. John had told Herod, "It is not lawful for you to have your brother's wife." And Herodias had a grudge against him and wanted to kill him. After his wife's daughter Salome danced before him, Herod publicly promised that she could have "whatever she asked" (Matthew 14:7). Prompted by her mother, Herodias, who was infuriated by John's condemnation of her marriage, the girl demanded the head of John the Baptist on a platter, and the unwilling Herod was forced by his oath to have John beheaded. Salome took the platter with John's head and gave it to her mother.

HEROD'S Actions:
Herod's Authority and John the Baptist's Imprisonment: Herod Antipas: Herod Antipas, a ruler of Galilee and Perea, had significant power

and authority. He imprisoned John the Baptist because John condemned Herod's marriage to Herodias, his brother Phillip's wife, as unlawful (Matthew 14:3-4, Mark 6:17-18).

Beheading of John the Baptist: Herodias Grudge: Herodias held a grudge against John for condemnation and wanted to kill him. However, Herod feared John, knowing he was a righteous and holy man, and kept him safe (Mark 6:19-20).

Herod's Birthday Banquet: During a banquet, Herodias' daughter, Salome, performed a dance that pleased Herod. In response, Herod rashly promised to give her anything she wanted, up to half his kingdom (Mark 6:21-23).

Salome's Request: Prompted by her mother, Salome asked for the head of John the Baptist on a platter. Though distressed, Herod complied to save face in front of his guests, and John was beheaded in prison (Mark 6:24-28).

How Sin Was Exposed: To kill the prophet, jealous Herodias bade her daughter, Salome, to dance for King Herod. The king was so entranced by her dance he offered to grant the girl any wish. John the Baptist was beheaded and his head was given to the queen on a platter.

Evidence: John's head served on a platter. Statement to the jury...Justice or Injustice?

Injustice
- Unlawful Execution: The beheading of John the Baptist was an act of grave injustice. John had committed no crime; his only "offense" speaking the truth about Herod's unlawful marriage.
- Abuse of Power: Herod abused his authority by ordering John's execution to satisfy a vengeful demand and protect his own pride and political image. This act violated the principles of justice and righteousness.

Judgment - The consequence of this action was multifaceted:

- Moral and Spiritual Consequence: The beheading of John the Baptist symbolized the persecution of the righteous and the suppression of truth by those in power. It showcased the moral corruption within Herod's court and the consequence of succumbing to personal desires over righteousness.

- Political Consequence: While there isn't a direct consequence mentioned in the biblical narrative for Herod, his involvement in the execution of John the Baptist could have impacted his reputation and political standing, especially among those who respected John as a prophet.
- Personal Guilt and Remorse: Herod is depicted as feeling guilt and remorse for his actions. He was haunted by the belief that Jesus was John the Baptist resurrected, indicating that the beheading continued to weigh heavily on his conscience.

Results of Abusing Authority

Personal Consequences for Herod: Guilt and Fear: After John's execution, Herod was troubled by guilt and fear. When he heard of Jesus' miracles, he feared that John had risen from the dead (Matthew 14:1-2; Mark 6:14-16).

Historical Consequences

Downfall and Exile: Herod's reign ended disastrously. He and Herodias were eventually exiled by the Roman Emperor Caligula. This exile marked a significant fall from power and prestige.

Biblical Perspective

<u>Divine Judgment:</u> The law often underscores that those who misuse their authority will face divine judgment. For example, Proverbs 6:16-19 lists behaviors the Lord detests, including shedding innocent blood and plotting well.

Overall, the beheading of John the Baptist by Herod Antipas was a clear at of injustice. It resulted from Herod's abuse of authority, driven by personal pride and the manipulative schemes of Herodias. The consequences of such abuse included a personal quilt, a historical downfall, loss of trust and respect, and a negative legacy.

Biblically, abusing power is condemned and ultimately subject to divine judgment, underscoring the moral responsibility of leaders to exercise their authority justly.

<u>God's Pet Peeve</u>: A heart that devises wicked schemes (plans).

<u>Jehovah Compound Names</u>: Shammah - God is There, Tsidkenu - Righteousness

Moral and Ethical:

This case offers several moral and ethical lessons:
Commitment to truth: John the Baptist's unwavering commitment to truth and righteousness, even in the face of opposition, serves as a powerful example. He fearlessly spoke out against corruption and injustice, regardless of the consequences.

1. Standing Against Injustice: His death highlights the reality that standing up against injustice and speaking truth to power can come with great personal sacrifice. John's beheading illustrates the dangers faced by those who challenge unjust authority.
2. Courage and Perseverance: John's steadfastness in his beliefs, even in the face of persecution, demonstrates the importance of courage and perseverance in upholding one's principles.
3. The Cost of Discipleship: The case underscores the cost of discipleship and the sacrifices that may be required in following one's faith. John paid the ultimate price for his dedication to his beliefs.
4. Legacy of Influence: Despite his tragic end, John the Baptist's life and message

continued to inspire and influence others, including Jesus Christ. His legacy serves as a reminder of the lasting impact that individuals can have, even in the face of adversity.

5. Moral and Ethical Implications:
6. Our ministry is never to be used as a weapon, only as a tool for the upbuilding of God's Kingdom.
7. Erosion of Trust: Abusing authority leads to a loss of trust and respect from subjects and peers. Herod's actions would have undermined any moral authority he might have had.
8. Negative Legacy: Herod's legacy is tainted by his actions. He is often remembered more for his unjust execution of John the Baptist than for his governance.

Overall, the case of John the Baptist's beheading encourages reflection on themes of truth, justice, courage, and the enduring legacy of those who remain faithful to their convictions.

Acts 3:19, "Repent, then, and turn to God, so that your sins may be wiped out, that times of refreshing may come from the Lord."

Guilty

Prayer: Father God, you are a God of your word. Your promises are true. Your Word gives me hope. You promise that when I repent you will faithfully wipe out my sins and refresh me in the Lord. I confess my sins, whether known or unknown, and am heartily sorry for them. I humbly ask for your forgiveness and the right path each day. Keep the Word of the Lord alive in my heart as I follow you all the days of my life in Jesus' name. Amen

No Matter How Committed Sin Will Be Exposed!

CASE # 10 - In Secret - Ananias & Sapphira

- People who conceal their sins will not prosper; but if they confess and turn from them, they will suggest that the best thing to do with sins is to confess them and put them out of one's life.
- He who conceals his sins will not prosper. But whoever confesses and renounces them will find mercy.
- People who want to admit when they are wrong have no desire to be right.
- REMEMBER, you can always walk away. The game ends when you stop playing.

Case #10: Ananias & Sapphira

KINGDOM OF GOD COURT

Give in Truth	District of	Prophet's Land

Kingdom of God	vs	Judgement in a Criminal Case

Ananias & Sapphira		#10

Title & Section	Nature of Offense	Count
Ex 20:15	Stealing	1
Prov 6:17	Lying	1

CASE DOCKET #10 - In Secret - Ananias and Sapphira

The devil has always had one key strategy when targeting the heart of mankind: lies and deception.

His reach is globally exponential when you consider the fact that he is the 'god of this world' and that anything and everyone that is NOT of God is under his direct influence. Since Satan's favorite weapon to use against us is lies and deception, the only way to counter him is with the truth.

<u>Text</u>: Acts 5:1-10

<u>The LAW</u>: (It is written) - Thou Shalt not steal. (Exodus 20:15)

<u>Sin</u>: A lying tongue, and stealing from God "Ananias, how did Satan get you to lie to the Holy and secretly keep back part of the price of the field? Before you sold it, it was all yours, and after you sold it, the money was yours to do with as you wished. So, what got you to pull a trick like this?"

<u>How Sin Was Committed</u>: Ananias and Sapphira's sin of deceit and hypocrisy concerning the sale of their land. In the New Testament, it is recorded that they sold a piece of property but conspired together to withhold part of the proceeds for themselves while presenting the rest to the apostles as the full amount. They wanted to appear as generous contributors to the early Christian

community while holding back some of the money for their gain.

How Sin Was Exposed: They were guilty and felt ashamed. Their sin was exposed when the Apostles confronted Ananias and Sapphira about the deceit.

Evidence: Their sin was not holding back part of the proceeds but lying about it, attempting to deceive the community and God.

Judgment: Ananias had not lied to man but to God. Because of his actions, Ananias died on the spot and was carried out. Later, when Sapphira arrived separately, Peter questioned her about the sale of the land and the amount they had received. She also lied and upon hearing the truth from Peter, she fell dead as well.

God's Pet Peeve: A Lying Tongue

Jehovah Compound Name: Tsidkenu - Righteousness

Moral and Ethical: Their deaths were a warning to the early Christian community about the seriousness of deceit and hypocrisy in dealing with God and others. We cannot guard against lies and deception if we don't know the truth and we can't know the truth if we don't spend time reading the word of God. The less truth we know, the more we will be deceived.

The naive or experienced person [is easily misled and] believes every word he hears, but the prudent man [is discreet and astute and] considers well where he is going. Proverb 14:15 AMP

Ananias and Sapphira teach several moral and ethical lessons:

1. Honesty and Integrity: The importance of honesty and truthfulness in dealing with others and oneself. Ananias and Sapphira's downfall came from their deception and dishonesty.

2. Transparency in interpersonal relationships and with communities. Concealing information or being deceptive can lead to harmful consequences.

3. Accountability: Understanding that actions have consequences and being accountable for one's choices. They faced severe consequences for their deceitful actions.

4. Generosity and Sharing: The value of generosity and selflessness in helping others. Their sin was not keeping part of the

proceeds but pretending to be more generous than they were.

Overall, the case underscores the importance of honesty, integrity, transparency, accountability, and genuine generosity in personal and communal life.

2 Corinthians 7:9-10a, "As it is, I rejoice, not because you were grieved, but because you were grieved into repenting. For you felt a godly grief so that you suffered no loss through us. For godly grief produces a repentance that leads to salvation without regret."

Prayer: Father God, I give thanks unto you for working in me godly grief that produces true repentance that leads to eternal life. It is easy to follow the wrong path of worldly repentance where I am only sorry that I got caught. Continue to give me a willing spirit toward good deeds and serving others in your glorious name. My specific prayer is that you remove every thought or intention of my heart that does not draw me closer to you in Jesus' name. Amen

No Matter How Committed Sin Will Be Exposed!

The Verdict

Conclusion of the Cases

In Conclusion, the court has meticulously examined the evidence presented (in all ten cases) and rendered its verdict of GUILT for all parties involved. While justice may be a harsh truth, we must confront the consequences of our actions. Let this verdict serve as a reminder that accountability knows no exceptions, and the law applies equally to all. With that, I rest my case.

Worldly Sorrow Vs Godly Sorrow

In all thy getting, get an understanding. Although, both are known as sorrow...it is important to recognize the difference between these two kinds of repentance to determine whether you are offering genuine repentance to God or another person.

Worldly Sorrow: Worldly sorrow tends to focus on regret over the consequences of behavior. It says, "I am sorry I got caught. I am sorry to face the consequences for what I did." It is sorrow over the consequences you face instead of sorrow over the hurt you have inflicted.

Worldly sorrow is self-centered; it focuses on the suffering of "poor little me" as you face the consequences of your actions. "Yes, I did that, but now nobody trusts me anymore. Everybody talks about me. Everybody is mad at me." Me is a key

word with worldly sorrow. Worldly grief produces death - 2 Corinthians 7:10b

Godly Sorrow:
Godly sorrow says, "I am sorry for who I have become. I am sorry that I have become so deceptive and dishonest. I am sorry for how my behavior has hurt you and destroyed our relationship." This is the difference.

Godly sorrow owns up to the sin and focuses on how to repair the damage, inviting repentance and restitution. That is why the Bible says godly sorrow leads to salvation and freedom.

A person who exhibits godly sorrow is determined to walk away from the behavior and move toward repairing the damaged relationship.

God's Mercy:
In His mercy, God did not dismiss your sins as inconsequential. Rather, He added them to the weight of sin His Son bore on the cross for you, and He remembers them no more.

When you separate God from vengeance and justice, the cross becomes superfluous. And the cross is anything but superfluous.

100

"But God, being rich in mercy, because of the great love with which He loved us, even when we were dead in our trespasses, made us alive together with Christ, by grace, you have been saved." Ephesians 2:4-5.

Psalm 103:12, "As far as the east is from the west, so far has he removed our transgression from us." Let us remember that it is easy to spend your days pointing out other people's sins and shortcomings. Instead, try spending time asking God to search your heart to convict you of your sin and keep you humble.

As a son of God, following God's commandments (LAWS) and seeking the will of God are cornerstones to intimacy with Him.

If by chance, you have a hard time confessing sins, remember that his great compassion and love always welcome you into the presence of the Lord. God's plan for your life is perfect. Lean in!

An Opportunity for REPENTANCE:

Beloved,
John 8:31, 32 (AMP) says, "If You abide in My word you are truly my disciples. And you will know the Truth, and the Truth will set you free"
Hence, I exhort you to take hold of God's Word, plant it deep in your heart, and according to 2 Corinthians 3:18, as you look into God's Word, you will be transformed into the image of Jesus Christ.

Join me in this repentance prayer so real, lasting peace through a relationship with Jesus Christ can be yours today.

God loves you and wants you to experience peace and eternal life, abundant and eternal.

Romans 5:1, "We have peace with God through our Lord Jesus Christ."

John 3:16, "For God so loved the world that He gave His one and only Son, that whoever believes in Him should not perish but have eternal life."
John 10:10, "Jesus came that we may have life more abundantly."

Guilty

God created us in His image to have an abundant life. He did not make us robots to automatically love and obey Him. God gave us a will and freedom of choice. We choose to disobey God and go our own willful way. We still make this choice today. This results in separation from God.

Romans 3:23 says, "For all have sinned and fall short of the glory of God."

Romans 6:23 says, "For the wages of sin is death, but the gift of God is eternal life in Christ Jesus our Lord."

Our choice results in separation from God. People have tried in many ways to bridge this gap between themselves and God. "There is a way that seems right to a man, but its end is the way to death." Proverbs 14:12

"But your iniquities have made a separation between you and your God, and your sins have hidden His face from you so that He does not hear." Isaiah 59:2

Jesus Christ died on the cross and rose from the grave. He paid the penalty for our sins and bridged the gap between God and people.

"For there is one God, and there is one mediator between God and men, the man Christ Jesus." I Timothy 2:5

"For Christ also suffered once for sins, the righteous for the unrighteous, that He might bring us to God." 1 Peter 3:18

"But God shows His love for us in that while we were still sinners, Christ died for us." Romans 5:8

We must trust Jesus Christ as Lord and Savior and receive Him by personal invitation. "Behold I stand at the door and knock. If anyone hears My voice and opens the door. I will come into him and eat with him, and he with me." Revelation 3:20

"But to all who did receive Him, who believed in His name, He gave the right to become children of god." John 1:12

Last, "If you confess with your mouth that Jesus is Lord and believe in your hearts that God raised HIM FROM THE DEAD YOU WILL BE SAVED." Romans 10:9

Follow these guidelines before closing with prayer: Admit your need (I am a sinner).

Be willing to turn from your sins; repent and ask for God's forgiveness.

Believe that Jesus Christ died for you on the cross and rose from the grave.

Through prayer invite Jesus Christ to come in and control your life through the Holy Spirit. (Receive Jesus as Lord and Savior)

Closing Prayer:
Our Almighty Living, True, and All-knowing God, I know I am a sinner. I want to turn from my sins and ask for Your forgiveness. I believe that Jesus Christ is Your Son. I believe He died for my sins and that You raised Him to life. I want Him to come into my heart and take control of my life. I am willing to make Jesus my choice, trust Jesus as my Savior, and follow Him as my Lord from this day forward, In Jesus' Name. Amen.

About the Author

The Spiritual View of Her

How Can This Ecology Puzzle Fit into the Ecosystem?
These puzzle pieces include prayer, love, forgiveness, loyalty, trustworthiness, submission, protocol, understanding, holiness, teachable, humility, empathy, character, covering, respect, sonship, ethics, morals, and values... The attributes of God are specific characteristics of God. According to her belief, these key attributes are standards of God that qualify one to stand before God's people and deliver a message from God.

God called Elder Patricia Durden Johnson into the FIVEFOLD ministry as a TEACHER. Teaching is her  ministry, both spiritually and naturally (these two correlate excellently together). When she teaches, she does not use her tool as a weapon. Instead, she uses it to uplift students' character and self-esteem. She strives to develop the 'total child' by correlating the attributes listed above. The physical, mental, social, emotional, spiritual, and financial aspects of individuals need natural and spiritual growth. Even so, she knows each setting is never the same. Hence, she is guided by the Holy Spirit to fully charge the curriculum into her setting. (Within the local church, one must stay in line with the spirit of the house). Staying in alignment is vital.

Also, it is her belief she must be the first partaker of the fruit. She must lead by example, submissive

to leadership. Her relationship with God has caused her to know God's voice and follow His way. Along with her Apostle (Dr. Kenneth K, Law), she is "Following the King and Advancing the Kingdom of God."

In addition, she is filled with the Holy Ghost and Fire, baptized in Jesus' Name, and under the leadership of Dr. Apostle Kenneth K. Law of the Embassy Church in Fleming, GA. 5493 Coastal Hwy 31309 www.theemessylife.org.

Fresh Out of the Box - Make lasting memories as you spend precious parent-child time immersed in this interactive reading experience. Watch as their eyes light up with delight and their minds expand with every discovery. The Fresh Out the Box Children's Book is more than just a book – it's a gateway to learning, creativity, and endless fun.

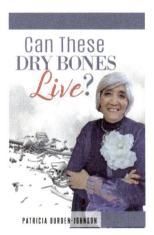

Can These Dry Bones Live? - Discover the power to defy life's darkest moments and rise again with "Can These Dry Bones Live?" Patricia shares her heroic journey of triumph over unimaginable challenges in this gripping book and reveals the secrets to reclaiming your strength, vitality, and joy. Brace yourself for a soul-stirring tale that will ignite your spirit and inspire you to respond with unwavering faith, just as Christ did. Unleash the healing power within your bones and unlock a life that defies all odds. Get your copy today and embrace the incredible possibilities that await you!

The Royal Telephone Directory - Introducing The Royal Telephone Directory Book – the ultimate guide to help teenagers and young adults deepen their relationship with Christ in a way that resonates with them. This interactive and engaging book takes readers on a transformative journey, breaking down the metaphoric relationship with God in an incredible and relatable manner.

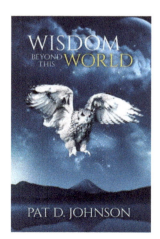

Wisdom Beyond This World - This is a must-read book for everyone seeking a wise and fulfilling life. This powerful book is filled with wise sayings and biblical advice that will help you navigate life's challenges. The book's core message is that "The fear of the Lord is the beginning of wisdom and the knowledge of the Holy One is understanding," which sets the tone for the entire book. These insights have been gathered from a variety of sources, including observation, experience, biblical knowledge, revelation, and faith. If you want to live a life of wisdom, then Wisdom Beyond This World is the book for you.

New Book Alert!!!
It Is Written

Get Started on Changing Your Life & Order Your Book(s) Today!

Contact Pat Durden Johnson for all booking events and orders at durden7johnson@gmail.com.